By Cynthia Macdonald

AMPUTATIONS   *1972*

TRANSPLANTS

For Phyllis,
    who knows a lot
about transplanting.
        Love,

        Cynthia

THE BRAZILLER SERIES OF POETRY
Richard Howard, General Editor

DISMANTLING THE SILENCE / CHARLES SIMIC / 1971

THE SENSE OF OCCASION / CHESTER KALLMAN / 1971

WELCOME EUMENIDES / ELEANOR ROSS TAYLOR / 1972

AMPUTATIONS / CYNTHIA MACDONALD / 1972

GOLDEN STATE / FRANK BIDART / 1973

WHOLE HORSE / KENNETH ROSEN / 1973

RETURN TO A PLACE LIT BY A GLASS OF MILK /
CHARLES SIMIC / 1974

A HOUSE OF MY OWN / CARL DENNIS / 1974

YELLOW FOR PERIL, BLACK FOR BEAUTIFUL /
TURNER CASSITY / 1975

THE PICNIC IN THE CEMETERY / CONSTANCE URDANG / 1975

TRANSPLANTS

POEMS BY

Cynthia Macdonald

Cynthia Macdonald
March, 1976

GEORGE BRAZILLER

New York

I wish to thank The National Endowment for the Arts for a grant which gave me time to work on this book, and Yaddo which, once again, proved a haven. I am grateful for the help Jonathan Greenwald (Dr. Dimity's colleague, though his antithesis) gave me with Dimity's medical vocabulary. And thanks to Don Harrell, Barbara Kellerman, John Unterecker and, especially, Jane Cooper for their careful, supportive criticism of the poems.

The quote on pages 16–17 is from Freedman, Kaplan, Sadock, Modern Synopsis of Comprehensive Textbook of Psychiatry, Williams and Wilkins, Baltimore, 1972; the quote on page 67 is from Grigson, Gibbs-Smith, eds., People, Places, and Things, The Waterly Book Co. Ltd, London, 1954.

"Thanksgiving in Cambridge, N.Y." was published in Moving Out. "A Story for a Child" was published in The Poetry Miscellany. "Cut Off" and "The Horns of Forgetfulness" were published in 13th Moon.

Library of Congress Cataloging in Publication Data
Macdonald, Cynthia.
  Transplants.
  The Braziller series of poetry.
  I. Title.
PS3563.A276T7   811".5'4   75-30732
ISBN 0-8076-0809-2
ISBN 0-8076-0810-6 pbk.

First Printing

Printed in the United States of America

Designed by Kathleen Carey

for Bill Cantrell

Contents

I

II (THE DR. DIMITY POEMS)

III

IV

V

I

THE STAINED GLASS WOMAN

The reason I fall apart easily
Is because they have not discovered
What can hold me together. Lead works
In window junction points, but not in joints.
Other metals are too inflexible. Rubber stretches.
Clay crumbles. Plastics
Are cut by the motion of my glass anxiety.

At the moment I am all in one piece. That is rare.
But then, I am rare. I must acknowledge that:
Glowing, refractive, transparent, colorful.
My mother kept putting pink on top of the other pieces
Until she realized that only made blue, lavender and
Yellow, orange.

Glowing, refractive, transparent, colorful;
Also unbending, fragile and sharp.
"She has a cutting wit," they say.
And I reply, "To wit, to woo; cuckoo, cuckoo,"
Trying to make light, as a stained glass woman should.

You knew how to do it, or, rather, did it without completely
Knowing how: made the heart beat, turning blood from blue
To red; made the sections fuse, annealing them; made glass
Into skin. There are no purple or green edges to cut you when
You hold me. Now when I move, I move in unison with myself,
Through places transformed by my transformation.

Only sometimes when the weather changes, or I am tired or angry
Or walk into a church or see a Tiffany lamp, I ache where
The seams once were. Then I am afraid that if you leave me,
A glassy residue may spread through me as quickly
And quietly as the rising light flushes a rose window.

III

You are gone. You were only
The preparation for someone else.
I walk accompanying the prepared space.
My food and furniture are glass.
I look at a glass landscape
And hear glass music.
I protect myself
With the material of myself.
That woman with blood
Reddening the water in the tub
Is the one who can be cut.
I will carry glass flowers to her grave.

MISTRESS MARY QUITE CONTRARY

"If the artist abandons himself to his feeling, color presently announces itself." GOETHE'S COLOR THEORY.

Because she had been born in February, the coldest month,
And in a cold house, the juggler had been
Perfecting her act since early childhood when she had kept
Two nipples from her bottles in the air at the same time.
She needed to, even though they had said not to,
And would not buy extras, and the shortage of milk
Made her bones soften.

Seven years after she had joined Ringling Bros.,
She was kissed by the ringmaster before she went on
To perform a new number for the first time:
Sixteen bells blindfolded while buried
In a tank of snow up to her neck. Using only
Her forearms and hands, she circled silver bells
To the arched sky. She felt them changing.
Color flowed through her fingers like blood
Returning after freezing. Taking off her blindfold
As they pulled her
Out to bow, she saw
The blue of hyacinths, the red of tulips,
The yellow of daffodils, the purple of iris, the green.
Spring had fallen into her hands. There was
No holding it back.

We are diagnosing the dream.
We have put it on the table,
Taken its pressures, measured its beats.

An exploratory is necessary.
We are anesthetizing the dream.
We are slitting its ripe belly.

We are performing an autopsy on the dream.
We have laid its organs out on the slab.
A perfect specimen.

We are reading the obituary of the dream.
It was widely beloved.
And celebrated.

We are visiting the grave of the dream.
Its tablet is bronze.
The lettering tells us what we already know.

The ribs of the dream close, caging our heads.
Our dreams are filled with the bones of desire.

THE STAINED GLASS MAN

for Donald Hirst

DRESDEN, OCTOBER 3RD 1928

Professor Oakes Ames
Director, Botanical Museum
Harvard University
Cambridge, Mass.

Dear Professor Ames, It seems easiest in this very long letter to separate the description of the glass work from the more personal part; so I have done this, and will tell you about the making of the models later. I have been out to Hosterwitz, half an hour by auto and have passed two whole afternoons, long ones, looking at the models. Then I inspected the work room and its contents and was shown all the great improvements made by the Blaschkas in the house since his marriage.

I have found, my dear Miss Ware, a new way of coloring the glass
Since you were here in 1908. I use no surface paint at all;
See this budding rose. You could leave it on the roof a year;
The shading would not change a micrometer. I know because I have
Done exactly that. The color is in the glass. Layer after
Layer I build it up. Not one, but many, like light itself.

> *I think he said he no longer paints at all except with the powdered colored glass which he can anneal.*

Here a sheet of cashew lake and one of violet beneath the luteous
Combine to form yellow of high intensity and brilliance,
A requirement of this liliaceous group. Their cups contain
The sun of early June, radiant, but with a touch of cooling blue.

I am covered with leaves. Leaves I have made.
They stick to me, annealed by the heat of
                    Loneliness. I am covered with glass
Of my own making. Leaves. The leavings.
        The parting. The final leaving. The left-overs.

The green of this ligulate corolla contains a drop of milk,
A happy accident, the accident for which a long apprenticeship
Prepares one. One day I ate, or at that moment drank would be
More accurate, my lunch while searching for a way to soften color
At the junction of the blade and petiole. You ascertain
The rest without the tale. You see the milky green.

*He is just as modest and honorable as he ever was, but now he
has a sense of his own worth, his own unusual force of intellect
and character; and there is everything to justify that.*

I regret this group of fungi is not complete for I can
Only do them as and when I can obtain the specimens.
My old gatherer died at sixty-eight three months ago and then
The new one died of tasting, though I warned him. The smuts and
    rusts
I grow here, but the mushrooms I must leave to someone else.

            Rusting. Rusting. Spores through skin.
    Molds forming skin. Molds.
                Molds stiffening. The marriage mold becomes
            The man. The armor.
        Clost to cupid's sound, but further than
    The new moon shining: a cutlass,
            A scimitar, a blade,
                    Slashing the air between us,
        Cutting, parting.

The molds are wonderful, and I think you will be delighted
with them all, but, of course, I know nothing of fungi.

The problem with Laver is it spoils when removed from the sea.
Its purples drain. It browns.
Fluidity becomes flaccidity. So I have had to work looking
Through the double barrier of glass and water. You would say
Both are clear, but clarity is an illusion.

Mr. Blaschka's head and bearing are very expressive and I wished
I could catch a photograph of his profile as he stood for a few
minutes, a plaque with a model on it held with both hands. His
whole expression of absorbed, concentrated study was worth
keeping, had it been possible.

Now, the land grasses. The lemma here, the lower bract—
Enclosing as it does the flowers in the spikelet of the grass—
Is smooth and tousled. I see a field of wheat within
This single stalk before me as I work.

        Transplanting them to the museum is
           The next-to-sharpest agony. Another
             Parting. Worse by far than
                The splinter of glass
                  Under the nail. It is the pain of sudden
      Feeling come too late. O, Lilianne,
           I dream you have not left.
                I keep the Boecklin *Flora* over the mantel.
    The keeping, the keeping. The dreaming.
              The parting.

You are most kind: supper and *Der Freischütz* are indeed
A lure. But I must put the next-to-final touch on the asparagus.
These stalklets will have lost their velvet by tomorrow.
Now the flowerets curve in like cat's claws holding to
The branch. There is a desperation of the parts within the flame.

*It troubles me very much that he and his wife cannot come over
to see his life's work now that you have the models so beautifully
arranged, and he looks so eager and pathetic when I describe
the mise en scène.*

This is the laver where I wash away the residues before
I trace the veins. Bronze. Because a brazen vessel clarifies
The light without refraction. Now, I will show you how
I do the leaf annealing. Cups of paraffin. I light them till
The flames drive at each other. This lever moves the apparatus.
The tips in first, then, bit by bit, the whole until it all turns
Red, as the after-image of a leaf stared at in sunlight.
And then the turning and the twisting for vein and edge.

   Lilianne, I tell this all to you.
    I speak to you whether I am silent
      Or talk aloud. The rest
   Is only the fragment of the whole. Like half
        A phrase of the Schubert we heard
   The night you left.
     Or like that single leaf. There.
      On the red crepe pillow.
         Single.
    The turning, the twisting.
   Single. The seeing. The parting.

*The strawberries were fascinating—plants, fruit and molds:
also the result of frost on the developing fruit.*

   The strawberries, my strawberries.
     Clustered like the nipples of Venus.
  Of Aphrodite. To suck. To bite.
    I picture babies crying at the case,
   Their milk need roused by my rosy artifacts.
      I picture you,

Lilianne, holding the baby.
Smiling. Rocking. Holding.

My last visit to Hosterwitz was most happy. Miss Niklason went with me and enjoyed it as much as I did. Supper was excellent, informal and pleasant, and I regaled them with all the Museum gossip I could think up. Mr. Blaschka did some leaf work again and Miss N. felt, just as I do, that it is a great experience to watch that man at work. His whole head and hands are a study, and he worked until it was about dark without turning on his electric light. She also felt that the work was enough to wear anyone's nerves to madness.

You said you would not have me.
Encased in glass. Encasing.
Now I make what I make from
The material of myself.
The leaving, the parting.
Then the loving.
Within my case I drown.
The leaving. The parting. The living.
Drawn out. Long drawn out. What works
Is work. Look at me.
It is all clear.

I know it has given him fresh courage to see me. I have been out there five times and I am sure that I accomplished what I came for. Please remember me to Louis and, with most cordial greetings to you and Mrs. Ames,
Very sincerely yours,
MARY LEE WARE

THE HORNS OF FORGETFULNESS

You said love should not hold such pain
So I washed it away in baths of *Moselblümchen* and pirouetted across
The garden into your arms, laughing.

You said you like women with uneven breasts
So I adapted a bicycle pump to puff the right one up and soaked
The left in boiling water to shrink it.

You said you were interested in astronomy
So I brought you a book with dark blue pages
And burning constellations.

You said you like women with humps because
There is adventure in cutting them open so I worked with weights
And pulleys until I grew a hill on my shoulder.

You said you would like to be with me more. But ... but ... but ...
You have too many commitments so I became a goat and used my
        horns
To butt you.

Now I am trying to stop bathing in wine,
Trying to even out my breasts, to burn up the sky,
To get rid of my hump.

As if the memorabilia were the memory.
But I need a sign on the fence around my field saying:
Please do not throw tin cans to the goat.

A SUSPENSE STORY

for Don Young

It was lucky he was so big or he would have had more trouble
With the black iron skillet he wore suspended from a chain around
His neck. Even so it tired him.

During the days he had been a minister, people often commented
That they had known those in his field to wear crosses,
But never frying pans. He smiled—even then,
Before his beard, looking more like Satan than Jesus—and told them
It had no religious significance.

It had been a wedding present from Mother, carried by hand
On the train from Wichita. When she died it was all
He had left of her so he hung it around his neck, close
To his heart. There it was that iron covering, that iron
Implement, that iron impediment, that iron memory.
It kept him a distance from love, but a distance
From pain, too. It hung there through a number of years
And three children.

One day when she'd clung to him, dragging him down once too
    often,
He hit his wife over the head with it. That knocked
Some sense into her: she divorced him and opened
A store called *Pairs*: whatever was—gloves, shoes, chopsticks,
Andirons—she had, except couples. Her partner
Is a woman.

He buried the pan and it is nourishing a pine—chelated
Iron keeps evergreens green—next to his front door. There is
A terrible weight gone from him. He no longer preaches
So he doesn't often moralize. But once in a while
He tells a client: I have a feeling it will all
Pan out in the end.

A STEP TOWARD BURIAL

You are presiding over the last rites of my marriage, helping me
     to bear my past and future.
         Will I live or die? You do not
Commit yourself. You give me a bundle, shaped like a baby,
     swaddled in gauze and tell me it
         holds the answer.
I begin to unwrap, hoping it will contain something of you,
     something I can hold or cradle. As the gauze
         unwinds, items drop out
Like plastic favors from a paper-wrapped surprise ball: one dollar
     at your local florist or party shop.
         I unwrap an inflatable rubber
Mother with air in her breasts and a narrow lap. I unwrap
     a typewriter with *I* on all the keys.
         I unwrap a son who can say
Only five words: do not leave me again. I unwrap a beating heart
     floating in a bottle—blood swirls
         through the glistening oil.
I unwrap a package of needles without eyes and a package of
     eyes without pupils. They
         cannot be used to study.
I unwrap clothes made of fat.
         I unwrap a statue of a father
     with a head guaranteed to grow grass
And a sign hanging around his neck: do not touch. I unwrap
     a daughter encased in mother-of-pearl
         from the waist down. I finish
The unwrapping. At the center there is only the center.
         The bundle
         did not contain
Something of you, something I could hold or cradle.

But you were right:
I have answered the question.

I take up the tangle of gauze and begin to prepare for burial
    by winding it around me, starting
    with my feet. The curve of
The ankle is difficult. At the armpits I realize I cannot
    continue. I will have to wait
    and ask you to complete
The bandaging, to bring me protection from the burning air.

THE AMHERST, HOUSTON,
NEW YORK TRIANGLE

I can wade grief—
Whole Pools of it—

> "Reactive" depression.
> Frequently tearful, seeking reassurance.

>> *And the slip, the drowning.*
>> *Usually unobtrusive.*

I'm used to that—
But the least push of Joy

> Precipitant usually obvious.
> Mood fluctuates, often at lowest point in evening.

>> *When you offer your hand,*
>> *I see the point of fingers: touching.*

Breaks up my feet—
And I tip—drunken—

> Motor retardation, rare.
> Somatic complaints vague, transient.
> Insomnia, if present, in early part of night.

>> *Checking your life-line for convergences*
>> *With mine, I find them present,*
>> *But will not try to penetrate prediction.*

Let no Pebble—smile—
T'was the new liquor—
That was all!

Power is only Pain—
Stranded, through Discipline,

Mood responsive to surroundings.
Vegetative signs mild or absent.

I will fix pudding for my dead father
And wait for signs in your next letter.

Till weights—will hang—
Give Balm to Giants—

Weight gain not uncommon.
Frequently tearful, seeking reassurance
Occurs throughout life cycle from adolescence on.

I wait, grief my "self-substantial fuel."
Sitting in a white dress and white bandages,
I send you an envelope containing:

And they'll wilt, like men—
Give Himmaleh—
They'll Carry—Him

A bird and a mountain.

SOURCES
The Collected Poems of Emily Dickinson, Modern Synopsis of Comprehensive Textbook of Psychiatry, Letter from CM to WAC

17

DIRECTION

Are you leading me further into the forest? Or out of it?
You are sure, anyway I will follow. That was clear when I saw
The trail you had left. Quails eggs. A favorite of mine
As well as yours. "We both see beneath the protective
Coloring," you had said, savouring them with the Chablis.
Your wife had taken the children to visit her six sisters.

I follow the trail, afraid, and sing to ward off danger.
    There's a long, long trail awinding
    Into the land of my dreams.
The air is swallowing the light; the pines are black.
(What's green and brown and black all over?)
I would like to turn back, but you egg me on.

I sing to ward off danger.
    I will not quail from mental strife,
    Nor shall my sword sleep in my hand, till . . .
Quail. Is that right? I did not bring my Blake along. When I get
To the end, will I find you? Or will the witch, angry that
You did not do as she instructed when she supervised your prayers,
Have baked you into a man? Or will I discover you are the witch or
Are married to her and that really all you wanted was
And au pair girl for the pair of you and your pair of children?
(A maid in the hand is worth two in the bush.)

I would sing to ward off danger if I could, but my mouth is full
Because I am eating the eggs, seasoning them with sweat. (Horses
Sweat, men perspire, ladies glow. I wish I did. It is so dark.)
I am eating the eggs, salting them away inside me.
I am thinking of the way your beard feels against my neck,
How your fingers curve over the arm of the blue chair.
Hold me. I am holding on. My hands are full of shells.

II

The Doctor Dimity Poems

for Hilda Bruch, Rollo May, Robert Seely,
Robert Walter

The laparotomy revealed a tumor of the insulin-secreting
Cells of the pancreas. Once the offending tumor had been
Removed, her behavior returned to normal and she was
Once again a dutiful, conscientious wife and mother.

The next case was much more difficult to diagnose—impossible
Three cardiologists before me said,
Three well-known cardiologists, that is. They knew the heart
Had been affected.
Well, any third-year student could have ascertained as much.
Even the parents could see their daughter
Turning bluer every day, like litmus paper when the moisture level
Changes. But all the films and graphs
And probes did not reveal the cause. I do not know what made me
Place my head against her chest exactly
As a doctor would have eighty years ago. But it is those unexpected
Bursts of inspiration which separate
The competent from the superior. My head against her breast.
It heard the faintest scratching,
Quite different from the rubs or murmurs we are trained to hear.
I strained to match sound with memory for
Several days. Oblivious to almost everything, I wore a sport shirt
To the office and asked
For "sandwich" instead of "scalpel" in a mitral valve replacement.
Then, in the kitchen on my third
Sleepless night, I got it or, rather, heard it; three scurried away
When I turned on the light.
She is alive and well, now, for it was simple to remove once
I had identified the problem.
Which orifice it entered through or how it lived within
A liquid medium we do not know.

Those are aspects which a class on diagnosis need not touch.

Next week I will discuss:
Life and the Liver in Sibling Kidney Transplant.

DR. DIMITY'S WIFE IN THE KITCHEN

Dr. Dimity's wife stirs the soup.
She is a mistress of the soup.
Her broth is the envy of her friends.
Her bisque is so delicious
She was named bisque cook of the month.
Her recipe for Potage St. Dimity
Is in the fifty-sixth edition of *The Joy of Soup*.
Now she is deglazing the roast pan.
She will greet Dr. Dimity with the soup.

DR. DIMITY'S WIFE GOES MARKETING

If I were a fat middle-aged woman (I am)
I would look at young, firm, thin girls
And pare myself into them (I do)
And I would attract young men with my ripe attractions (I do not)
Even though I would be afraid they would walk away (they would)
When they saw me naked (I am too afraid).
At the supermarket a fat middle-aged man gave me the eye
In the aisle between waxes, polishes and pre-soaks.
I gave it back to him. He looked surprised that anyone
As fat and middle-aged as I would spurn him (I did).

Although like most people I have a number of small failings
I have one major flaw. Really major, you could say;
It permeates my whole life-style. Or my whole life.
For is there a difference between life and style?
One's style is one; one is, one could say, one's style.

Anyway I have incorporated my flaw into myself
So that anyone who knows me well,
In fact, who knows me at all,
Notices it and I know
They have noticed.
I never mention it; so they never mention it.

There is absolutely nothing I would rather do,
That I do not already do, than to get rid of my flaw.
I mean it. At the same time I recognize that without it
I would have been almost too perfect: rich, intelligent,
Handsome, compassionate, friendly, well-informed, loyal,
A brilliant diagnostician, not only able to eat ambidexterously
With knife and fork or chopsticks, but having trained
My children to do so, too. My wife could never master the art.
Three cars, two beautiful daughters. Able to recite
Diseases of the Chest and Heart from memory, well-traveled,
An active member of the Planning and Zoning Board
And the *Chevaliers de Tastevin*. Well, one could go on,
But I am also modest and list my virtues only to emphasize
That through the whole which is the whole, the flaw pervades.

My wife, for whom the flaw is like a skin obscuring
Everything, spends almost all her time attempting
To peel it. That flaw is all that keeps us together.
I tell her that; she does not hear. She tries to remove it.

She does not seem to hear, but dabs more
Soup behind her ears and on her wrists as if it were perfume.

HOW DR. DIMITY DUCKED RESPONSIBILITY
TO SAVE HIS INHERITANCE

Dr. Dimity's father was the famous Dr. Dimity.
In 1924 he founded the Drake Infirmary.
In 1934 Dr. Dimity Jr. began his residency at the Drake Infirmary.
In 1935 Dr. Dimity Jr. noticed his father was going blind.
His father denied his infirmity.
He refused to retire. He kept on operating.
His son threatened to report him to the County Medical Society
But that would have risked the Infirmary;
That would have risked the inheritance.
So his son assisted him and tried to be his sight.
In 1936 a woman died when his father cut an artery he couldn't see.
In 1936 his father retired.
In 1936 his father died at the Albergo Fontina in Venice.
In 1946 Dr. Dimity was named director of the Drake Infirmary.

DR. DIMITY'S DIVE

Dr. Dimity has read an article on Scuba diving in *Holiday*.
He decides he and his girls should learn even though
Dorothy is afraid of deep water (stalled elevators,
The punishment closet, the car trunk when the key had been
Locked in), and Daisy is afraid of eels (rubbery boa constrictors,
Uncle Herbert's hugs, the turquoise ring which had to be cut off).

He makes reservations for Antigua and does Canadian Air Force
Exercises with them each morning, chiding them for their fears
Between: one, arms up; two, touch toes; three, hold breath; four . . .

In Antigua they have instruction and then are ready.
They move into the blue-green arena.
Dorothy discovers the water yields. She swims through it,
Leaning against it as if it were her lover,
Holding it between her thighs, feeling it enter.
Daisy discovers the water yields, does not encircle.
She sees sea lilies, blue and purple, anemones, fans of fronds,
Coral spawning sequined fish, and moves, delighted,
As if she were at Tiffany's.
Dr. Dimity feels the water leaching his oxygen, the coral
Slashing his arteries. He looks through his mask at his wrists,
Expecting what he does not deserve. There is only veined skin
And his waterproof Bulova. No laceration. Yet he knows
He will die if he continues. He motions his daughters, impatiently,
As if ashamed of their cowardice, and leads them deeper,
Flashing his perfect white smile.

DR. DIMITY'S WIFE'S SPECIAL DAY

It is Dr. Dimity's wife's day of despair.
She permits herself one day a week
And that only when he is at work.
She stays in her nightgown, gorging
On forbidden foods: translucent pear honey,
Barbecued oysters in sweet spiced juice,
Glacéed artichokes, green figs filled with lemon cream,
Peanut butter, until she must tie a string around her neck

To keep the delicacies down. Like a French farmer's
Goose. While she stuffs she watches
The Guiding Light, The Secret Storm, Search for Tomorrow
And *Love American Style.* She allows herself to admit
That she hates soup and would leave Dr. Dimity
If she knew how to do anything else.
The rest of the week she is what she refers to
As herself. Sometimes if she feels desperate too soon
She permits herself to oversalt the soup.

DR. DIMITY IS FORCED TO COMPLAIN

Dr. Dimity's head hurts. He refuses to use a stronger word.
He lies in his darkened bedroom, groaning, trying
To contain his pain. The smell of soup
Which permeates the house, even though his wife has
Turned off the stove, makes him feel worse.
He asks her to send for Dr. Doctor who cancels
His next two appointments and postpones his golf date.
Dr. Dimity, his friend and colleague, never complains.

Dr. Doctor begins with the eyes and needs look no further.
Through his opthalmoscope, instead of the usual vascular pattern
Radiating from the optic nerve, he sees straight
Horizontal lines of light. "I see
Straight horizontal lines of light," he tells Dr. Dimity
Who groans, trying not to shut his eyes.

"Wait, the lines are widening. There are slats between them.
It is a Venetian blind. Being pulled up. I am not sure

If I am looking out or looking in."
A storm, trees bending, breaking.
The sky is being ripped by wind. A house.
Grounds, bushes under water. It is moving fast,
Rising fast. Debris batters the house.
A man and a boy lean out the window, looking
At the rising water. The boy is crying.
Dr. Dimity shuts his eyes, "That is enough."

"It was like a nickelodeon," says Dr. Doctor.
"I would write this up for *Internal Medicine* if
I could make a diagnosis. I know you will agree physicians
Present the most baffling problems and
Are the least cooperative."
"A form of migraine," says Dr. Dimity.
"A flood of painful memories," says Dr. Doctor.

DR. DIMITY'S WIFE CHANGES MORE THAN HER NAME

Dr. Dimity's wife lives alone.
She uses her own name.
She no longer cooks food, only metal and wax.
She carves
Metal and wax figures.
Their fingers hold objects:
Scalpels, chopsticks, cruise brochures,
Golf clubs.

When she exhibits, she places
The bodies

In front of heaters. Her theaters.
The wax melts gradually. Vital
Parts drip to
The floor. The metal softens.
Bends. Folds.
He folds. A man's voice on tape repeats:
I am floored, floored,
Flawed.

When the show is over and those
Unsold
Have been returned to the loft,
She picks one,
At random, to sit in the wing chair,
Cold, metallic, with
Rivulets of wax extending
His angles,
Covering his openings.

After the six cartons of hot and sour
Ordered from the Peking Hut arrive,
She pours
The soup over him to soften
Him up.
In bed, she reshapes him to her satisfaction:
Testicles become breasts.
Penis, a second smile.
With a flood of pleasure,
She thrusts her finger in, making the vagina,
The eighth hole.

A big Victorian house: the drawing room is filled
With drawings of doors. The blue damask walls
Are hung with doors and there are more of them
Stacked on tables, leaning against the potted palms
And the mantel of the marble fireplace. Some are
Almost fully three-dimensional with real brass or
Silver handles; others are tentative crayon marks,
Suggesting doors only because they are surrounded by them.

Dorothy used to go to the drawing room to eat chocolates.
Or to play solitaire. Or to watch the crystal worlds
In the geodes. Or to read her future in the lines
Of the potted palms, even though the messages in plant
Capillaries were difficult to decipher. She knew
The room was full of doors; they were of little interest,
Part of the family furniture. But then, her father
Began to send her there: made her stay
Until she had learned her irregular verbs, made her stay
Until she had finished the cross-stitched place mat
For her mother's birthday, made her stay
Until she apologized because he'd lost his temper.

Later he became the one to apologize.
He would send her into the drawing room, would follow
Her in, shutting the doors, would put his head in her lap
As she sat in the red velvet chair, would ask her
To stroke his hair, to kiss his neck, to grant him
Forgiveness, would pick up her hands and press them to
His mouth as if to print his lips on her palms.
Surrounded by doors, he would whisper his adoration.

Now she chooses to go

29

To the drawing room. She sits in the red velvet chair
Trying to decide what to do about the doors,
Whether to buy locks to keep him out or keys to let him in.
She picks up a pen and draws a door on her palm.
She picks up a brush and paints a palm on a door.
She picks up the pack of cards and draws doors on
The back of each one. Dr. Dimity's daughter, Dorothy,
Has begun to deal with doors.

III

BIRTHDAY MESSAGE

I have no experience to go on in this situation
(I am like a child) and I begin to cry,
Brushing my teeth I cry, tears mixing with toothpaste.

no no nice beans first sunny so you are a big girl walk no no
not so far away once upon a custard spoon for Daddy do not touch
swans bite and another bite for Mummy is dust in the sun no no
clean up high in the sky you do not bite tin cups pinned to your
Dr. Denton's arms a big one for Granny we are almost to the swings
bang bang against the crib if Ginny broke Uncle Bernie no no
she was asleep and one for Nanny who no no you did it yourself
naughty

I cry tears mixing with the toothpaste.
I am so angry you can do this to me.
That I stick out my tongue at the mirror.

bad news for you guessed it I guess Ginny died today looking at
Easter flowers bloom in boxes under the ground in the park where
it is dark summer on an island alone with Daddy teaching
multiplication tables on Mummy resting to Granny afraid of mice
standing on the tables cook and man her husband cooking
Mlle. Lais smelling bad Uncle Bernie whose head had been
glued back on under the lake there are messages you could
understand if you could answer seven times eight you are one
going on the other apartment to escape memories of Ginny

I stick out my tongue at the mirror. The map
On my tongue gives me no sense of where to go
Or what to do. It is white with red roads and craters,
Ugly like so much of the rest of me.

read Swiss Family Robinson again you cannot use the public

library germs attack you anyway it is such a lovely day you
should be outside there are no children on the hilltop alone
you look at the brown brush hills catching fire and the rock
snakes sun on top of the hill there is such a lovely view of
Westwood and LA and UCLA and Venice is too far for a roller
coaster ride

My ugly tongue and the rest of me are forty-five
Today and what is happening is like starting over and
I do not think I can do that knowing, as I did not
Then, what is ahead or behind.

marry Colin sorry you do not like anyone I dance the rumba
without a father who has already married again and again I have
told you not to let the cats mess in the bathtub you examine
your breasts more pointed than your mother's always told you
how pretty you could be thin sunlight and the day leaks away
into the park without knowing how

Knowing what is ahead or behind I turn away
From the mirror to write you for a survival kit.
I will check each day for a message
Behind Ernst's drawing, "The Family
Is the Root of the Family." When
You reply, the directions will begin:
"If you can trust enough to love, the chance
Of hemorrhage is lessened. But if
There is a rupture, be careful.
Go to bed until you clot.
Repairs cannot take place under blood."

A STORY FOR A CHILD

The mushroom was beautiful.
Its pleats were as sharp and neat as
The folds of a half-closed silk fan.
Its skin was as smooth as the inside
Of a mouth. And it was resilient.
The gradations of tan to brown from
Edge to center were as subtle as those
On a color wheel, but had more depth.
Its setting of green moss and ferns was
Felicitous. It was fecund and dropped
Its spoors easily and freely. And
It was not aggressive. Its name,
Aminita Angelica was melodious.
All in all, the word for it was: perfection.
Unless what you wanted was an umbrella stand.

But it was more complicated than that if
What you were was a perfect mushroom yourself.
Consult *Snow White* for what would happen then. But
Remember that the happy ending was because
It was a story for a child.

DIFFICULT REVISION

I have written
            the story of my life   and now I
Am reading it to find out what happened.   Mother interrupted
        Her trip   to the Andrews' anniversary gala
                (which she always
    Enjoyed celebrating because   they were such an unhappy couple)
        when   it was time for
                    my birth.
She called them   to say she and Father would be late
    because they had to go home to dump her   bucket of Daphneas.
    Father asked her
                if she shouldn't stay at the apartment
                                    to care for
The fleas   but she said   that's why I hired   the nurse.

    Mother came to the nursery
                            almost   every day   for at least
Half an hour to see how our training was going. She even learned
    All our names: D, Da, Daph, Aph, Phnea,
                            Nea and Ea and
    Could tell us apart   most of the time   particularly when
                    she used the
                magnifying glass.
But finally   she decided that trying to distinguish
        Who was who was   just too much trouble   and she had the
                    nurse
    Put our names in spangles
                        on our overalls and bibs.
                                The nurse followed
Mother's instructions though she did not   need the names
                                    herself.

Then comes a part
            I could not write;   you can call it
Writer's block, call it neurosis, call it whatever you like; so I do
        Not know what   occurred   for about two years.
                                    The place where I
    Am able to take up the narrative again   was after
                            the circus
            was already in
Operation   each afternoon   in the living room of our Park
        Avenue apartment.   Mother would be in her apricot tea gown
    serving tea
                from her great grandmother's silver service
                                        to the audience
(Carefully selected so we would not catch anything from them. Nea
Had died some time before and Mother was convinced she had caught
Whatever it was from a member of the teatime crowd.)
        We went
                    through our routines.   I was at   the bottom
            In the Tower of Flea act   but got to wear
    A beautiful red satin outfit. And later   in the trapeze part
                            I was
        The star.   The spotlight which the butler worked was on me
                        alone as I
                did five sommersaults
Before being caught   by D and Da.   Often a member
    Of the audience   was so enchanted by my grace   he or she
Threw a bit of
                cheese and marmalade
                                or watercress tea sandwich
In the cage.   I guess they did not know   we lived on blood.

37

I turn the page. We have all become elephants. My name
Has been changed to Phany. We are still in the circus
Doing the same tricks, but they no longer fit. Mother
Has leased the Roxy for her teas so there will be room for the show
Which she has retitled: Elphantasy. You can see that
I was central. One day during The Tower of Elephants,
The stage collapsed. We fell, a shower of splintered beams and
Elephants to the concrete basement. As I was at
The bottom of the tower I was at the bottom of the pile.

In the hospital
There has been ample time
To finish the story of my life,
But when I regained consciousness
I vowed not to continue
Reading unless I could rewrite.
And that is difficult
Because I am encased in bandages,
Immobilized by pulleys.
Yesterday the doctor
Gave me his hand. That's when
I noticed
I had one.
A hand.

ACCOMPLISHMENTS

I painted a picture—green sky—and showed it to my mother.
She said that's nice, I guess.
So I painted another holding the paintbrush in my teeth,
Look, Ma, no hands. And she said
I guess someone would admire that if they knew
How you did it and they were interested in painting which I am not.

I played clarinet solo in Gounod's Clarinet Concerto
With the Buffalo Philharmonic. Mother came to listen and said
That's nice, I guess.
So I played it with the Boston Symphony,
Lying on my back and using my toes,
Look, Ma, no hands. And she said
I guess someone would admire that if they knew
How you did it and they were interested in music which I am not.

I made an almond soufflé and served it to my mother.
She said, that's nice, I guess.
So I made another, beating it with my breath,
Serving it with my elbows,
Look, Ma, no hands. And she said
I guess someone would admire that if they knew
How you did it and they were interested in eating which I am not.

So I sterilized my wrists, performed the amputation, threw away
My hands and went to my mother, but before I could say
Look, Ma, no hands, she said
I have a present for you and insisted I try on
The blue kid gloves to make sure they were the right size.

Today I saw it: Ed Carmel died

And I became the world's biggest man. O, the years I have waited . . .
Ever since . . . it must have been when I was ten and he was twelve
   That I first heard of him.

There was a piece in the Oswego News about a Brooklyn boy who was a little
Over seven feet and weighed three hundred pounds. That's when the rivalry
   Began, at least for me. I do not know

Exactly when he heard of the Wisconsin Peak, as I am known.
Our family name, you see, is Peak. A noble name and one which lent
   Itself to sloganeering in the days

When I was on the road: Peek at Peak, the Mammoth Freak.
Ed, too, was on the road, but not in tents. He had a Rock group:
   Frankenstein and the Brain Surgeons, a catchy name.

One time in Tuscaloosa I saw that he was playing and called him up
And asked if he would like to meet for dinner, but he said
   The truck he used to haul himself around

Had broken down and so he couldn't make it. Some other time, he said.
I really would have liked to see him, to have known how it would feel

To be smaller than someone. And yet
Today I celebrate. I am the biggest now in the whole world.
I never made nine feet as he did; I stopped at eight foot, ten.
     Never made his weight, either, although
I guess I could have, but I feel better just about four-twenty-five,
Give or take thirty pounds or two plus stone. I like the English way
     Of saying stones, the sense of being
Made of boulders. His obit says his grandfather, at seven feet, was called
The tallest rabbi in the world. Well, mine was called the tallest butcher
     In Wisconsin. When I heard the news that Ed was dead
I felt a rush of loneliness and then of joy. If you must be big
Then biggest is the best. Or so I used to think. That if
     I were the first, the biggest
Then I would be there, would have arrived, but now . . . I think I'll call
Kentucky Fried and say send over a barrel of the Colonel's best
     For the world's biggest man.

41

INNARD LIFE

for Beverly Guster

There are three things important to me in life,
My trinity of needs. Unfortunately, I have
Forgotten what they are. I know there are three
Because I have recited them so often, using
My fingers to make sure I have remembered each one.
Now only the numbering remains. Remains, remains
To be buried in the shallow graves I dig: numbers are thin.
One certainly has something to do with you: you will go away
And leave me; then I will go away and leave you.
I blame you for both leavings, but that is not the answer.
I stand beside the graves and concentrate on thinking
Of your eyes, but all that I receive is: two.

Three witches (worn-out symbols, but
One cannot choose one's saviors or persecutors.
They look worn-out, too: bags under their eyes and
Over their hearts) walk by and grant me three wishes provided
I can name them in three minutes. But, of course, I cannot
Remember what I want or need and the effort makes me feel
Myself falling. "Hold me up," I call to them; so they
Whip out their pistols and demand, "Your money or your
Life." I give them the currency I have down to
The last 8¢ stamp, but they want my life, too.
They slice me open and pull out my organs which
Play Bach fugues, alternating with skating rink selections.
Then they walk off, red with blood and money,
Festooned with kidneys, heart, lungs and intestines.

IN PREPARATION

A discovery! A discovery! Christopher Columbus has not
Just sailed across *her* stomach though he would certainly
Have found it round not flat. He has not had to steer
The Niña, the Pinta and the Santa Lucia, whose hoarsman is
A Venetian, past the abyss of her navel which (with the change
Of a single letter if he speaks English) refers to his whole
Endeavor, because *she* is not the whole world.

A discovery! A discovery! Mme. Curie assisted by
Pierre who has kept her lip stiff throughout the travail,
Though they do not yet realize their tripe à la mode de Caen
Is radioactive, will not inhabit *her* bones to create
The skeletal tour de force (or however you might phrase it
In French) because *she* is not the whole world.

There will be earthquakes even when *she* is asleep and did
Not stamp a foot or slam a door. Some bad smells
Are caused by the oil refineries. It will rain when *she*
Smiles, and so forth: she is no longer *she.*

She reaches toward the ceiling, her sky at the moment,
And calls, "O, Vasco da Gama, come to me;
Now I am ready to set sail with you, to plunge into
Those foamy billows I used to think were made by
My own saliva, to swirl into the whirlpools,
No longer the black circles of my ear holes."

"O, Newton, My Isaac, come,
Lunge upon me from the apple tree
And I will fall with you to earth,
Demonstrating gravity in a swoon of passion."

She picks an ember out of her tear duct
And amber out of her cunt
And sits down, all unstoppered, to wait.

JASON OF WHOM I AM A PART

Jason, do you feel the exact moment I
Enter your room each night,
Feel me slipping into your bed before
I wrap myself around you, sucking you dry of juices?
I know I am there long before I am there.

Jason, tell me the exact moment you know I am there,
Filling the sockets of your eyes
And the tunnels of your ears with oil
To replace the drier juices I have drained away
So that we slide together into warm seas, overlapping.

We force ourselves to peel away the layers of the sea,
To emerge, because I must always leave before morning
Or the light will slice us apart and maim us,
Like Siamese twins after the operation has been botched.

Separated, we pull on our daytime latex,
We pour coffee and go to work
And move through the day as if it existed,
Waiting for the night. Jason, tell me
The exact moment you know I am there.

SEVERANCE PAY

She decided the best place to meet him again was
Joe's Meyerland Barbershop where he went for his haircuts.
He had told her that much about his regular life. So she
Sat vigil in the waiting section.
When the owner noticed she had been there over an hour
And was not getting a cut or meeting a husband or son,
He questioned her. They worked it out: for ten dollars a week
And her agreement to vacate if the chair was needed,
She could sit as long as she wanted.
A week passed and he had not come.

At first she limited herself to six hours a day and tried
To keep things going at home, but because she was so distracted,
The house began to fall apart: the wallpaper separated
From the wall, the milk curdled as soon as it was delivered,
Mold grew on the dishes and furniture. And the people wore down
Or out. She decided she would rather put all that behind her
And make permanent arrangements to stay at Joe's.
Two weeks passed and he had not come.

There was plenty of time to read and she filled in her gaps
By going cover to cover through Playboy, Penthouse,
Popular Mechanics, Esquire, Readers Digest, Holiday,
Psychology Today and Western Horseman. However, she could not
Do nothing but read so she began to watch the barbering
Then tried her hand at it. Customers
Started to request her, especially for head and neck massage.
The third and fourth weeks passed and he had not come.

Then, at 6:30, on May 7th, 1973, she saw him framed behind:
JOE'S—MON—SAT—8 AM—6:30 PM

46

He looked surprised, though she did not know whether it was because
He was surprised to see her, in view of the way
They had parted, or surprised to see her shaving Mr. Parriot.
Wait, she indicated and he did, though he seemed worried
About the time. She told him not to,
She'd stay late and take him anyway.

To the forty-eight positions of love described in
The Infinite Varieties of Bliss and the ninety-four
in *Up, Down, Sideways and Backwards*, they added one. The angle
Of the barber chair produced exquisite sensations, especially
After such a long hiatus. Again and again they tried and
Succeeded in different chairs. Finally he yawned
And she said: Sleep; I'll give you your haircut and a massage
Right there.

When he woke it was morning.
Delilah was turning the pages of *True Confessions,*
Smiling. She had already swept up the curly brown and grey hair
And put it in the discard pail,
Which would serve her as a locket.

IV

INHERITANCE

I see my mother's last breath
Which has not been drawn
In pen and ink, its jagged graph scrawled on my face,
Crossing out my features
With her lines.
Her lines come out of my mouth so that I discuss
The appearance of the neighbor's children,
The dirty streets of New York
And love, in the same tone of smooth disapproval.
Disapproval sours
My skin into hers,
Implants her congealed brown eyes, her long nose to
Look down, her lips
Like the edges of oysters.

Once a day I sandpaper my features. The swelling
Has obliterated both of us. The basin
On my lap catches our common blood.

A DISCREET PLOT

White dotted swiss with wide pleated
collar and ruffles on the hem, white
cotton undershirt and underpants,
white lace-trimmed slip, white cotton
stockings, white elastic garters,
flat white shoes with single strap
and button closing, pink bow in long
dark hair. Even at twelve, she knew
that white did not become her and
longed to wear the orange Spanish
shawl which covered the piano.

She rode her bike until a feeling
Made her dismount and lie face down in
The skunk cabbages which
In later years she thought of as Queen Ann's Lace,

White silk jersey, draped in Grecian
folds, white lace and silk under-
pants, white garter belt, pale silk
stockings, silver sandals with four
inch heels, filagree diamond brace-
let, graduated pearls, platinum
wedding ring, dark hair, short,
curled in a circle away from the face.
Her daughter told her she looked
beautiful in it so she bought the
first white dress she'd owned since
her wedding.

After he had taken off her clothes, leaving her
Dressed only in her pearls, she lay face down, impaled on him,
Rotating slowly on the weathervane of his expectations,
Which in later years she thought of as his folly.

White 50% dacron, 50% cotton seer-
sucker, round-necked, open down the
back, three ties to close opening,
long white hair tied in a purple
ribbon, gold wedding ring. She
said she was as thin as when she was
a girl and that her breasts were
disappearing so she'd have to get a
bra from the pre-teen department.

Connected by tubes to the hanging bottles
She could not lie face down, but she ran her fingers
Through her pubic hair, remembering. In later years,
Continuous care of the plot was covered by her bequest.

INVESTITURE

Mother's room:

I drop my clothes on the floor as if I were
The child, reproached by governesses, who were
Reproached by her for permitting such disorder.
Undress for bed and dress for it.
I need a nightgown. Pull open drawers:
Stockings, scarves, sweaters.
Here: a whole drawer of silk.
Try one. Then all. Arrange in piles
Of those too small and those that fit.
Count: fifty-three . . . between our ages.
Check the mirror for flattery.
Decide which to keep.
Not too many; she may miss them if she comes home.
She may miss them somehow anyway, may know that
They are gone and who has taken them.
I choose six, put them in my suitcase.
But I will sleep in one now:
White crepe trimmed with turquoise.
Her nightgown invests me with
The grace of a long neck,
The ability to tango,
The indolent allure of legs
Thin enough to cross at knee *and* ankle.
The air smells of lilacs and I slip
Through it, seducing it, whirling
In the white and turquoise nightgown,
My breasts supported by her straps.

White caps bubble on the blue carpet.
They bracelet my ankles as I dance.

The sea is rising. I whirl; the water,
Deepening, tugs at me. I push through it,
Dancing, dragging my heavy thighs.
Water is drowning the bed,
But it floats
Because it is wood.
I float because I am fat,
Weigh twice as much as
My mother whose bones
Attack her skin.
I cannot continue the dance, weighted
By wet turquoise and white silk. I cling
To the bed, the skin on my fingers, toes, nipples
Pleating in the water. I pull myself onto
The wet mattress and float into chafed sleep.

After washing to remove the night's sharp salt,
I take Mother the three nightgowns
She asked for yesterday:
"Not too short, to protect me
From the hospital sheets,
Cotton because it is hot here,
The smallest because I am so thin."
I show her an extra,
White and turquoise, she might
No longer want because it is so big,
Might want to give to me
Because I am so big.
"No," she says, tying the strings of
Her lace bed jacket more tightly,
"That is a favorite." I fold it and
Put it with the others by her bed.
I will have it soon.

THE LATE MOTHER

One, two, Buckle my shoe
      To go to Boston.
      The phone call said she was going:
      "She can't last long," but
      The buckle has come off my shoe.
Three, four, Close the door.
      Thread the needle.
      There are tears and I am getting
      Far-sighted.
      Try again.
      Knot the thread and sew the buckle on.
Five, six, Pick up sticks.
      Five years ago she almost set the bed on fire,
      Hiding her cigarette under the blanket
      When the surgeon came.
      He took out her lung.
      I have sewn the buckle on backwards.
      Is she puffing away now, blowing
      Smoke out of her tracheotomy tube
      Like the billboard man
      Who steamed rings over Times Square?
Seven, eight, Don't be late.
      I am ripping off the buckle.
      As soon as I finish I will go.
      I will not be late for the dying. Probably.
      The thread knots binding me to my place.
      My father said to her, "We are going to be late
      For the dinner party." Then she said it
      To her next husband, as if
      The going out must be a struggle.
Nine, ten, Big, fat hen,
      Warm and feathery,

A nest of softness.
Never was, could not be,
"Teach her to tie her shoes, Mademoiselle.
She can't seem to learn and I must
Dress for the dinner party."
The buckle is on.
I keep the needle threaded in case.

The rhyme is over.
We must leave the nursery
But we are afraid.
I hold her, eighty pounds, in my arms,
Becoming her mother and my own.

THANKSGIVING IN CAMBRIDGE, N.Y.

for Susan Crile

Last night I slept in a flies' graveyard, a second floor room
In the farmhouse of a friend. No one had been there
Since summer. The floors and walls were decorated with flies
In various stages of ascent from earth to heaven.
They were stuck to the ceiling, thick as stars;
There were even constellations, including small clusters of
Dead copulators. About to turn out the light,
I saw movement: one fly was still alive,
Crawling on the white ruffled curtain which was
Studded with so many of its kind.
I was too tired to sweep them away
And fell asleep hoping I would not dream nightflies.

I am here with three friends. Jules is limping, afraid
His gout will climb to his heart. Susie wonders if giving up
Smoking will kill her. Her lungs feel worse.
She has just spent two weeks getting less air
Than she could sip through a straw.
Laura tells us she almost drove into
The rear of a truck when she fell asleep driving up here.
The hood of her car was under the truck when she woke.
I am afraid of leaving my son, afraid one of us
Will die because I would not stay.
Five bottles of red wine stand on the table,
Waiting for the feast. I take the Turkish shawl
Off the couch, put it over my head and
Read palms. All our life lines
Flicker. It is impossible to tell which one of us
Will crawl alone on the white curtain.

V

THE EEL AS THE LETTER E

The Eel lights the water and zigs through it.
Its consciousness of itself has made it
Into a kite, cutting the sky into angles,
Until the lightning hits it, electrifies it.
Look, look at the plankton revealed in its head-
Lights and the green matrix of its survival. It
Is green, not because of reflection—the depth
Is too great—it is green because of content.
The plankton divide every twelve seconds and
Their increase would leave no room for the water if
They were not devoured. The eel sifts them
Through his teeth as he zags through his colored sky.

At the Rokanjii we are served skewered livers
First, then marinated flesh in raw slices,
Then grilled fillets, then bunches of brains on rice.
All eel. This restaurant celebrates the eel by eating it.
Afterwards in the elevator of
The Tokyo Tower we ascend through the ocean—blue—
And generate lightning between our hands.

TURNING

It took seven months to make that bowl,
Much more beautiful than any I had made before.
You helped me by looking at each one,
Admiring the roughness of those intended to be rough,
The translucence of those intended to be seen through,
Suggesting changes in the shape or glazes
And giving me a basket for discards.

So I made this one, the most perfect, for you,
Starting with the sand-colored earth near the river
Which curves its protective half-circle around our house:
I mixed in cast-off fragments of shell for texture,
The juice of iris leaves for color,
Flakes of mica for glint, waves from Amagansett inlet
For undulation, the fluids of my body for love.
And the shaping, the shaping, the caressing,
The scratching, the gouging until the bowl
Looked as stark as a moonscape, as
Astonishing as a dark sky suddenly studded with fire-
Works, as rough and strong as granite,
As yielding as water,
As green as frog skin over all the other colors
Which change with the season and the giver.

I had to give it to you, wanted to;
It was made for you. Even though I knew that
My father had thrown my present, a pickle jar covered with
A bright kaleidoscope of papers, into the incinerator
And my aunt had coughed
When she burned the scented candle I had made in school.
I held the bowl out to you: the force of my caring
Too much broke it before you could.

We continue to walk barefoot on the shards
Which we cannot sweep up because of what they contain.

MAKING IT UP

All those scenes of passion are set by the ocean,
  Waves crash at the dissolve, the couple fades into
   Foam. So I have decided to place our meeting in the
    Desert which, as I have never been able to spell, I spell
     Dessert. Uncertain which one I have gotten because out here
      In the Sahara there are no dictionaries, I settle for a
       Date sundae with hot grit in the whipped cream and
      Lie down to await you who are over there taking
Off your pith helmet, I guess.
                    Dolly in, dolly in.
But, as I mentioned previously, I have a problem
  Spelling and so my abracadabras work no better than candelabras.
                    Cut. Number two light is out.
    You do not appear, with or without your pith helmet.
     I would have taken you either way, although
      The pithy is hard to chew. But, dates
     Are, too. So here I am, dark brown and
Sticky, attracting the sand flies.
                    Wardrobe. Button her blouse.
I consider approaching the camel to hump, but decide
  Instead to concentrate harder, which must be successful
   Because your hand emerges from beneath the prone camel followed
                    Make-up. Darken the hand.
    By the rest of you. What a body! I can see it even though you
   Are coated with sand. We come together, moving toward abrasive
                    Zoom in.
Bliss when a wave washes over us. The transports of passion
Are easily dissolved by too fine a focus.

THE STORY OF MY DETACHED RETINA
AND ITS EFFECTS

How did it happen? That is what everyone asks, that is,
That is what everyone asks who knows about it.
I was leaning over in the shower to see the leg I was
Shaving and I sneezed and the screen at
The back of one eye ripped. Of course
I did not know that that
Had happened then. I saw a black space
And blinked and dried my face and kept blinking.
But the space remained and what I saw was blurred.

Later in Houston, Dr. Whitney Cohen, *The Eye Only*,
Said they could have lazed the retina together.
But in Eola they are not well-informed
About the finer points of eyes. So now I am
One-eyed, in terms of vision, though both
Are still embedded in my head. You want
To know what it is like, this single seeing?
Cover one eye. The doctors say
That all you lose is depth perception
And insurance against blindness.
They are correct about the loss. The gain
Is what they do not seem to understand.
I can see into the centers of cabbages
And tell which ones contain babies and which of them
Will become princes and which frogs. I can see
Through blue to the color on the opposite side.
I can distinguish those who are two-faced from those
Who are only wall-eyed, something Picasso
Could never do. I can see which of the girls
Playing cowboy will become nurses and which hairdressers.

I can see through green to the heart of money.
I can see the hypotenuse in a hypothesis
And can thus pinpoint the best place
To start the scavenger hunt. And then
I can announce which team will win because I can tell
Exactly where and how to get
The pear-shaped pearl from the Sultan's turban
And the iron nail from a newly shod donkey.
I can see into red and read blood messages. I can see
Which waves will grow to sweep away towns and time
My visits to the beach perfectly.
I can see into poems until
The words dissolve and there is no more
Need to write them, the page
Becomes blank, a field of snow
Into which I walk and lie down, closing
Both the seeing and unseeing eye, no longer
Needing to distinguish which is which.

THE PRESENT

A tree, very often an oak (which was a sacred tree) was split in two,
the lower part hollowed out like a trough to hold the corpse, the
upper part served as a cover.

He brought me a present: a wooden Indian hollowed out
Like a body, hinged in halves. It was painted the colors
Of sea shallows on a bright day, a persimmon, coal,
A chameleon on moss. It was lined in the underfur of seal.
When the wind leaked through the cracks of my house,
Chilling the rooms until they sweated and the rims
Of the rocking chair froze to the floor, I'd close
Myself inside: the Indian would hold onto me.

This special form has been explained by two ancient beliefs:
1) Men were supposed to have grown out of trees.

He took it back, put it in his truck, saying, "I wish
I could let you keep it." I tried to use what I had learned,
Tried to say he needed his own present, but when the cold
Cracked the pitcher on my table and splinters of milk
Patterned the cloth, I drove to his house and, in the dark,
Painted on his door: INDIAN GIVER. I stand behind that.

2) The "tree of the dead" is very much like a dugout, and it may
therefore have been considered appropriate for the last journey
"across the water." The newly dead were believed to be in an inter-
mediate state between life and death, still possessing a certain aware-
ness of what happened to their bodies.

So when he nears the door, he will hear me
Breathe. When he puts his hand on the knob, he will
Feel my pulse. And he will know me in the warp of his house.

67

A GIVEN

"Homage kills. God talks to no one, and imposes on us his image of loneliness and anger." PENELOPE MORTIMER

It killed the girl who drowned in his eyes.
It killed the boy who followed him across
The Mohave on a motorcycle.
It killed the woman, but not quite enough
So she walks around staining the carpets
With her leaking embalming fluid.
It killed him. He smothered beneath
The quilts of their homage and
Emerged a garbage collector.

God talks to no one.
He mumbles in a regional accent so
No one can hear him clearly.
He plays chess by himself.
He writes articles on
The death of the girl,
The boy, the woman
And describes his own funeral so movingly
He cries as he puts on his uniform at 4 A.M.
To go on his rounds, mumbling.

And imposes on us his image of loneliness and anger,
Which we reimpose on ourselves.
The girl practices her dives, preening
Like a ballerina *en pointe*,
The boy works summers for five years
To buy his cycle,
The woman refuses to take out death insurance.
He wraps the garbage in quilts and tries
To give it away.

LOOKING INTO MY FATHER'S HOUSE

for Jennifer Tim Macdonald

I have had to drive by your house almost every day
To find out how things were going, to discover how I was doing.
At first I went at night because I thought I could look in
And you would not be able to look out. But the curtains
Were drawn, the windows bright, blank rectangles
And all I could see were the smeared lines
The white pillars made against the brick, the STP stickers
On your son's windows and the empty shelves in the garage.
As usual you were concealing what was inside.

> It is dangerous here for me.
> On this street there are knives
> Hanging from the trees.

So I began to ride past at dusk, the time
When lights are needed and the shift from day to night
Has not yet nudged the occupants to close the outside out.
There was more risk for me—no longer invisible—
And so I wore disguises: a large straw hat, dark glasses or
A veil. But I do not think you would have known me anyway.
One day I forgot my instruments of disguise.
Your daughter walked by the parked car and stared,
Then hurried into the house to tell whoever was inside
That she had met an old dream of herself.

> It is dangerous here for me.
> The knives hang, pointing down,
> Glinting sharply in the street light.

I had not seen inside until last night.
The day was stormy so at six, the time I have arrived
The last few weeks, the dusk had turned to black.

The large window in the living room was
Unconcealed and there we were,
Sitting around the gold-tooled leather game table,
Playing (if that word can be used when
All the faces in the game were puffed with anger).
You and your daughter argued. The anger

Seemed to grow; your face became mottled and veined.
The mother turned from one opponent to the other,
Fluttering placations. The brother crawled under the table,
Smiling. Your daughter screamed something at you,
Stamped her foot and left. I could tell
From the way you watched her go
That she would have to stay in her room until
She apologized. Then the mother closed the curtains.
Tomorrow night I will have to come again. I do not want to
But I have nowhere else to go. I will have to come again
To see if I can see inside.

         It is dangerous for me here.
         There ares knives hanging by stems
         From the branches. If the anger
         In the house escapes its confines
         They could be shaken loose
         To slice down,
         Severing me from my past,
         Cutting off my present.